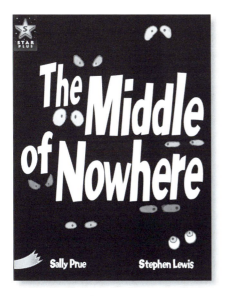

The front cover

Where is 'the middle of nowhere'?

What feeling is the illustrator trying to create?

The back cover

Let's read the blurb together.

Do you think the family are going to enjoy their holiday?

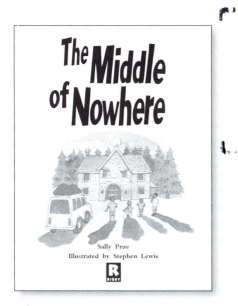

The title page

What does the picture show?

What do you think Mum is thinking?

Lesson 1 (Chapter 1)

READ

Read pages 2 to 4

Purpose: To identify the narrator of the story.

PAUSE

Pause at page 4

Why do you think Mum wanted a peaceful holiday?

Why do the children think it sounds boring?

Where do you think they usually went on holiday?

Chapter 1

My family always argued about holidays.
We always wanted to go to different places.
I always wanted to go to Funworld. Ben always
wanted to go to Water Mania.

"Not this year," Dad would say.

We usually ended up going where Dad
wanted to go.

This year, Dad said, "It's Mum's turn
to choose."

Ben and I were very surprised and excited.
Until Mum said, "I'd like to go somewhere
nice and quiet. Somewhere right in the
middle of nowhere."

"Oh, no!" said Ben and I. "That sounds
so boring!"

3

"We'll stay in an old house," said Mum.
"Somewhere with no traffic and no television."

"Well, maybe just a small television," said
Dad. "But somewhere peaceful."

"Yes," said Mum. "A nice, quiet house
in the middle of nowhere."

And that is exactly where we went.

4

READ

Read pages 5 to 9

Purpose: To find out what surprises await them in the middle of nowhere.

PAUSE

Pause at page 9

Why does Ben wish he was back at home?

Look at the simile used to describe the house on page 7. (*the door looked like an angry mouth*) Ask the children to describe something else about the house, using a simile. (*e.g. it was as dark as a cave*)

Did Mum know they would have to use candles? Find evidence in the text.

It was a long way to the middle of nowhere, and we all got hot and grumpy.
"I wish I was back at home," said Ben.
"So do I," said Dad.

5

We drove on and on. The road got narrower and narrower. Large, dark trees cast shadows across the road.

At last, Mum stopped the car, and we all climbed out.

"Where are we?" asked Ben.

"The middle of nowhere," I said.

We had stopped outside an old house in the middle of a forest. The windows of the house were dark. The door looked like an angry mouth.

"It looks boring," said Ben, with a gulp. "Let's go home."

CANDLES ON THE TABLE

Mum opened the door with a big iron key. It was quite dark inside.

"Where's the light switch?" asked Dad.

"There's no electricity," said Mum, when we'd looked all around the room.

"How can we watch the television?" asked Dad.

"How will we see when it gets dark?" asked Ben.

"That's easy," I said. "Candles!"

READ

Read pages 10 to 14

Purpose: To find out what else was wrong with the house.

PAUSE

Pause at page 14

What made Dad change his mind about the house?

Why did the children think their holiday wasn't going to be boring?

What do you think will happen in the morning? Will they decide to go home? How might things get better?

Please turn to page 14 for Revisit and Respond activities.

There was a black pot hanging over the fire, but there was no oven anywhere.

"Isn't this exciting?" said Dad.

Mum didn't seem so sure. Ben definitely didn't seem sure. And Dad didn't seem sure, either, when he found out we could only have bread and cheese for tea.

By then it was really dark, so we lit some candles and went to our bedrooms.

Mum and Dad's room was big and creaky. Our room was not so big, but it was much creakier. The flame from the candle made black shadows jump around scarily on the walls.

I'm sure Ben was just as scared as I was, but neither of us said so.

10

11

The bathroom was even worse. It was full of dark holes where spiders could hide. Or frogs, or toads.

"Or even striped snakes with big fangs," said Ben. "I don't think I need to go to the bathroom."

12

It was cold in bed, so we wore all our clothes. The wind moaned around the house.

"What if something comes down the chimney?" asked Ben.

"It won't," said Dad.

"But what if it does?"

"It *won't*," said Dad, and he blew out our candle.

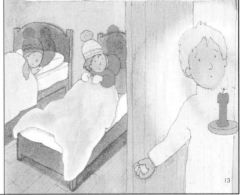

13

"Molly!" said Ben.

"What?" I asked.

"It's very creaky."

"But not boring," I said.

"No," said Ben. His voice wavered.

A flash of lightning lit up the room. Thunder rumbled.

"Definitely not boring," he said.

14

Lesson 2 (Chapter 2)

RECAP

Recap lesson 1

Whose idea was it to go to the middle of nowhere?

What did the family find when they got there?

Ask the children to describe the house.

READ

Read pages 15 to 18

Purpose: To see if things were better in the morning.

PAUSE

Pause at page 18

Why didn't the children want to play hide-and-seek?

Why did Mum think they were being silly?

What do you think might happen next?

Ben and I tried playing cards . . . and
I-Spy . . . and board games..
    "This is boring," I said.
    "There's nothing to do," said Ben.
    "Why don't you play hide-and-seek?"
asked Dad, again.

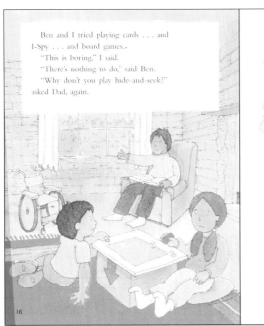

"What if the spiders get us?" asked Ben.
"Or the striped snakes?" I said.
"You could rub Mum's face cream all over
you," said Dad. "That tastes horrible. Nothing
will eat you then."

    Ben and I went to find Mum, but she
said we couldn't have any face cream. She
even told us to stop acting so silly!
    That made us so upset that we didn't watch
where we were going. We went left instead
of right at the end of the hall.

READ

Read pages 19 to 21

Purpose: To find out what the children found.

PAUSE

Pause at page 21

How do the children feel? How do you know?
(*frightened, knees knocking*)

Why do the children decide to open the door?

Would you open it?

What do you think they will find?

"This is wrong," I said. We were in a narrow hallway. It was even darker and gloomier than the rest of the house, and I felt a bit frightened.

There was a deer's head on the wall, and at the end of the hall was a little door.

"I don't remember that before," I said.

"What's that noise?" asked Ben suddenly.

"It's your knees knocking," I said.

The little door was very dark, and almost too small for a grown-up.

"What do you think is on the other side?" I asked.

"Snakes," said Ben. "I wish I had Mum's face cream on."

"We have to find out," I said. "If it's something horrible, it might come and get us while we're asleep."

"In the middle of the night, in the middle of nowhere!" cried Ben. "And that would be the end of us!"

READ

Read pages 22 to the end

Purpose: To find out what was behind the door.

PAUSE

Pause at page 24

Ask a child to read aloud the opening paragraph on page 22. What word does the author use to show that the children were scared? (*slowly*) Why is the word repeated three times? What other words could you use here to give the same effect? (*timidly, cautiously*)

Why do the family decide to go back next year?

Slowly, we went up to the door. Slowly, we pulled the handle. Slowly, the door creaked open.

We looked. We couldn't believe our eyes!

"Mum!" we shouted. "Dad!"

We had found the door to the back of the house.

"Look at the lake!" said Mum.

"We can go swimming and fishing!" I said.

"Look at the cabin and the swings!" said Ben.

"What a great place for a barbecue!" said Dad.

22

23

And you know, we had so much fun on that holiday that we all agreed to go back to the middle of nowhere again next year!

24

After Reading

Revisit and Respond

Lesson 1

T Look at the narrator's thought bubbles on pages 2 and 3. Ask the children to describe the different holiday settings. Which one looks the most exciting?

T Ask the children to find the words and phrases that the author has used to describe the house. (*middle of a forest, dark, creaky, black shadows*) Talk about how the author creates a picture of the setting in the reader's mind.

W What other words would you use to describe the house? (*spooky, mysterious, scary, creepy*)

Lesson 2

T) How does the setting change at the end of the story? The author doesn't describe the new setting in detail, instead we see it in pictures. Ask the children to suggest words and phrases to describe the picture on page 24. (*sunny, relaxing, fun, peaceful*)

Follow-up

Independent Group Activity Work

This book is accompanied by two photocopy masters, one with a reading focus, and one with a writing focus, which support the main teaching objectives of this book. The photocopy masters can be found in the Planning and Assessment Guide.

PCM 7 (*reading*)

PCM 8 (*writing*)

Writing

Guided writing: Produce a brochure to advertise a holiday in the middle of nowhere. Use PCM 8.

Extended writing: Write a short recount about a holiday you have had.

Assessment Points

Assess that the children have learnt the main teaching points of the book by checking that they can:

- discuss story settings, and locate key words and phrases
- understand how story settings influence events and behaviour
- use synonyms and other alternative words.